SURPRISED BY JACK

——•——

*An Introduction to the Life
and Works of C. S. Lewis*

BOB HEREFORD

ISBN 978-1-0980-3796-3 (paperback)
ISBN 978-1-0980-3797-0 (digital)

Christian Faith Publishing, Inc.
832 Park Avenue
Meadville, PA 16335
www.christianfaithpublishing.com

Printed in the United States of America

"Little Lea" Lewis's childhood home in Ireland

Patricia, for all your help, encouragement and support.

Illustrations by Kent Hereford (excluding cover)

CONTENTS

PREFACE

"He was the meekest and lowliest of all the sons of men yet he spoke of coming on the clouds of heaven with the glory of God. He was so austere that evil spirits and demons cried out in terror at his coming, yet he was so genial and winsome and approachable that the children loved to play with him, and little ones nestled in his arms. His presence at the innocent gaiety of a village wedding was like the presence of sunshine.

"No one was half so compassionate to sinners, yet no one ever spoke such scorching words about sin. A bruised reed he would not break, his whole life was love, yet on one occasion he demanded of the Pharisees how they ever expected to escape the damnation of Hell. He was a dreamer of dreams and a seer of visions, yet for stark realism He has all of our stark realists soundly beaten. He was a servant of all, washing the disciples' feet, yet masterfully He strode into the Temple, and the hucksters and moneychangers fell over one another to get away from the mad rush and the fire they saw blazing in His eyes.

"He saved others, yet at the last himself he did not save. There is nothing in history like the union of contrasts which confronts us in the gospels. The mystery of Jesus is the mystery of divine personality."
—James Stewart, theologian, 1896–1990

What is the use of studying the works of an Oxford professor who admitted to being a dinosaur over sixty years ago? His opinion, on some points, would be ridiculed in much of Christendom today. However, C. S. Lewis's beliefs about the Christian faith reflect a better picture of what Christians have believed for centuries than the teachings of the best and brightest of current Christian theologians. There is nothing new in Lewis's description of what Christians have believed for two centuries. They may seem new simply because they are no longer expressed.

Lewis's works should be studied today because there are uncountable Christians who have never heard of logical reasons to believe, nor have they ever heard the arguments of nonbelievers being tested. Our well-meaning clergy, many times, assume a level of understanding in the congregation they speak to each Sunday that does not exist. There is an ever-increasing problem for the message of sound historic theology to be heard. Lewis gives us a complete array of levels of understanding on a myriad of subjects. I hope you come to the banquet and taste.

In *The Screwtape Letters*, C. S. Lewis warned us that "Christianity with a difference" is what Satan wants to be proclaimed. Lewis, through *Screwtape*, told us that "the horror of the same old thing" is what is used against the believer. Consequently, we are always trying to reinvent Christianity. We are always trying to produce something different and unique while all along, we celebrate the most unique thing that ever occurred—the entrance of an infinite God into finite human time and history.

This desire for change expresses itself in many different ways. It is usually directed toward the fashion of the day. Consequently, the church continually becomes more conformed to the culture than the other way around. The culture is influencing the church of Christ in dramatic ways. From the acceptance and celebration of same-sex marriage to the promise of prosperity, much of the church of today would be almost unrecognizable to Lewis.

Jack Nicklaus, the great golfer, said that when his golf game was suffering, he always went back to check the fundamentals of his swing. He said that usually, there was something wrong with the basics that was causing the problem in his game. Today, many golfers create a completely new swing rather than seeing what is wrong with the basics. The church of Christ is trying to create a new faith. In many cases today, we witness a faith that denies or does not proclaim the basic tenants that have been observed for over two thousand years. As Lewis put it, we are now the accusers of God, not the other way around. We require answers from him, not he from us. We have put God on the witness stand. As Lewis phrased it in an essay sixty years ago, God is now in the dock (on the witness stand), not us. Today, we believe God is here for our pleasure. The Christians of old believed we were created for his pleasure.

Once again, we are trying to put God in a box. But God, revealed through the humanity and divinity of Jesus, is much more complex.

As James Stewart wrote, "The personality of Christ is a mystery." One only has to look at the deaths of the Apostles to see that there is much more to Christianity than prosperity and celebration of sin. Even at the time of his Son's most critical need, God turned his back.

Lewis immerses us in the reality of what Christians believe. It is a place between almost all behaviors are okay, and God exists to make you rich. His word to us is to take up our cross and follow him, not to believe so one can prosper or give license to all behavior. He is a God who prefers one type of behavior over another.

Lewis said in *The Screwtape Letters* that the devil's goal is to have us doing the opposite of what the age we live in needs the church to do. The devil wants us using fire extinguishers in a flood and telling everyone in a boat that is about to sink to run to the side of the boat that is already almost completely underwater.

So when the biblical view of marriage is being trampled by the culture, some in the church believe we might as well celebrate same-sex marriage rather than explaining and defending the concept of Christian marriage, as it has been viewed for centuries.

Even when we have prosperity in a way and magnitude that would be unrecognizable just two generations ago, we have a portion of the church saying that it is not enough. God is at your service to provide even more.

The philosopher Friedrich Nietzsche proclaimed that "God is dead!" The modern church, rather than kill him, has tried to enslave God. We want to make God our servant—to be at our beckon call for ourselves and the approval of our actions.

The *Mere Christianity*, expounded in all of Lewis's writings is a wonderful antidote for the fashions of the day, religious as well as secular. As Lewis believed, and I agree, there is no such thing as a new morality. New moralities and new religions generally come from hucksters or crackpots.

Lewis's message is simple. We are sinners saved by the birth, crucifixion, and resurrection of God's Son. The fact that belief will do you well on this earth is possible but a minor point in reasons to believe. We should believe, as the catechism suggests, to glorify God because it is the chief purpose of man. It is not to get rich or give one permission for almost any activity.

I am told that the preface of a book is used to tell the reader why a book was written. What was the motivation of the author? This is a good exercise not only for the reader but perhaps even more for the writer.

My reason for writing this book is very simple. I want the reader to read more of the works of C. S. Lewis. His books defend and explain the faith. The simple message of grace, as Lewis said, "That is what it is and was what it was long before I was born and whether I liked it or not." I have tried to write a book I wish I had available to me after I first discovered C.S. Lewis.

Lewis's autobiography is titled *Surprised by Joy*. His fascination with joy and his search for truth were key ingredients in his coming to faith. Likewise, I was surprised by the writings of Lewis, which helped my faith and my view of the world.

Lewis did not care for his given names, Clive and Staples. At age four in honor of his dog who had died, he declared his name to be Jacksie. It was shortened to Jack. He was called Jack by friends and family from then on. I pray that the writings of C. S. Lewis are as useful to you as they were to me. And that the story of his life will be inspiring as well. You may be as "Surprised by Jack" as I was.

INTRODUCTION

C. S. Lewis—probably the greatest defender of the Christian faith of the twentieth century—was, until the age of thirty-one, an avowed atheist. However, less than a decade after his conversion to Christianity, he was asked by the British Broadcast Corporation (BBC) to produce a series of radio talks explaining "what Christians believe" to a British population enduring the height of the German bombing of London and England. What an ironic picture. There was Lewis, explaining the Gospel of peace to an audience suffering death and destruction at the hands of a maniac determined to rule the world.

The series of broadcasts, as unlikely as it may seem, proved to be very popular. The broadcasts were made into three booklets. A decade later, they became a book titled *Mere Christianity*. The book was one of the bestselling Christian works of the twentieth century. Its popularity is still evidenced today, with sales topping one hundred thousand a year.

I am thankful to God that the BBC and Mr. Lewis got together. I encountered *Mere Christianity* and Professor Lewis in a bookstore on vacation in 1988, forty-seven years after the broadcasts and twenty-five years after Lewis's death. *Mere Christianity* was the only religious book in the store (at the time, I thought it an accident).

After I read the introduction by Charles Colson and the chapter he first heard read to him, "The Great Sin," I was hooked. If you read no further in *Surprised by Jack*, at least read the chapter "The Great Sin" in *Mere Christianity*. I read *Mere Christianity* in its entirety that week, and I have never looked at the world or my beliefs as a Christian in the same way. I agree with Charles Colson. "It is the book God has used most powerfully in my life apart from his own Word."

Soon, I began reading anything I could find written by or about Lewis. I was amazed at the amount of material Lewis had written in all different genres—children's stories, science fiction, novels, essays, and sermons, not to mention scholarly works and of course, his apologetics (his defense of Christianity). What was so appealing to me about Lewis's writing is that he was not reluctant to take on almost any subject. After reading Lewis for thirty years, I also count his writings as the single most important part of my overall education. My introduction to Lewis made me realize how uneducated I was. I believe I got from him most of the traditional "classic" education I missed in school.

Some people tell me Lewis is too hard to understand. I disagree. His analogies are simple and easily grasped. His logic and prose are concise and clear. Parts of his apologetic writing that may appear difficult are the parts that attempt to explain difficult things about our faith—things we don't understand or we don't accept. Lewis believed that the hardest things about our faith are exactly the ones we need to study most. Scientists, he always said, study first the hardest things to explain. His first apologetic works, *Miracles* and *The Problem of Pain*, are perfect examples of taking on the hardest and most asked questions about our faith.

In *Mere Christianity*, for instance, he explained and defended the basic beliefs held by Christians down through the ages. One reason for my writing this book is to share his explanations and defenses of the faith. Lewis never said he had all the answers. I would run from anyone who even seemed to believe they understood completely all the mysteries of our faith. What Lewis gave us were reasonable explanations about our faith and a reasonable defense as well.

At no time do we need to hear that "defense" more than now. I am confident Lewis would be amused, astonished, amazed, and angered at the state of the Christian church today.

I was confirmed in the United Methodist Church at the age of nine and attended church regularly all my life. I was thirty-eight the summer I read *Mere Christianity*. I had never heard the arguments for belief that were so well-articulated by Lewis—not in Sunday school, not from the pulpit, nor in youth programs. I never heard logic and reason as arguments for belief. Lewis believed that if Christianity is true, it will ring true in all of reality. He believed we are always being tempted to leave logic out of our defense of Christianity.

In one of Lewis's most popular books, *The Screwtape Letters*, the senior tempter, Screwtape, warns his apprentice, Wormwood, to keep his patient away from argument and logic because he is playing to God's strength. "Don't worry about what is true or false," he told Wormwood; all they want to know is what is "practical" or "contemporary" or as we do today ask the question, "Are we on the right side of history (whatever that means and more importantly how will we ever know)?" I would say the tempter has done a great job eliminating reality, logic, and commonsense from our proclamation of the Gospel.

Of course, Lewis's arguments are not the foundation of belief; however, when belief is shaken, they serve as a reminder of what one has accepted as true, no matter how one may feel. Also, Lewis's arguments are a great inoculation for new believers, especially for young people who are faced with conflicting views and opinions at every turn.

In one chapter in *Mere Christianity*, "The Shocking Alternative," Lewis addressed questions I had wrestled with all my life: free will (Why did God give us free will?); the fall of man (What caused it?); the Christian view of history (Why does mankind always mess things up, no matter how hard we try?); and the deity of Christ (Why he can't be *just* a great moral teacher?). He wrote about these subjects clearly, concisely, and logically, all in less than two thousand words.

In *Mere Christianity*, Lewis also pointed to the evidence of an absolute universal moral law that suggests there must be a lawgiver. All these arguments do not prove the existence of God and the deity of Christ, but they can help move us along our way to a stronger faith. Lewis's arguments make our leap of faith a much shorter jump.

His arguments also give us a logical, defensible reason for our faith. In fact, one of the critical mistakes of Christian clergy, Lewis believed, was that "foolish preachers" have made a mistake by telling us Christianity is a sure formula that will help us in this world.

The idea that Christianity should be followed because it will do you good and our country good is a common appeal of the church today. Christianity should be recommended for one reason only in Lewis' opinion—it is true.

Lewis had a dim view of those who proclaimed the Gospel for worldly success or became believers because they hope for answered prayers. In one essay, "The Efficacy of Prayer," he wrote about answered and unanswered requests to God. He uses Christ as the ultimate example. He wondered why we should expect our prayers to be answered when he refused his Son's request for help at his most anguished moment. As usual, he turned the table on the reader and suggested that if our requests are sometimes answered, we should not make too much of it because if we were stronger, we might not be treated so well. In fact, we may be sent to face harder battles with far less help.

And make no mistake, Lewis believed we are in a battle. That idea is almost completely gone in major Christian thought today. Although renouncing the "powers of evil" is required as a statement of faith to join the United Methodist Church, you will hardly hear evil or the devil mentioned from any pulpit. In *Mere Christianity*, the prevalent theme of Christianity is, as Lewis puts it, living in "enemy occupied territory."

Besides looking at major themes in Lewis's work, we will also review his life, with emphasis on his journey from atheism to belief. Many have called this quest a search for "joy and truth." These were the two major factors that propelled and sustained his search. Lewis was also helped to faith by friends, and books, and new ideas. One such idea was "chronological snobbery."

Chronological snobbery is a simple yet profound notion. Simply put, it is the recognition that we stop believing in things or stop doing things not because they were ever proven wrong or not useful but because they simply went out of fashion. The Spirit of the day found them lacking. Many parts of our Christian practice and belief have been abandoned because the culture finds them out of fashion, not because they were, in fact, wrong. I believe it also implies that old ideas, morals, and faith are rendered false just because of their age.

After a long struggle with his atheism, Lewis finally determined that atheism is just too simple. As he wrote in *Mere Christianity*, his argument against God was that the world was so unfair. But he asked where he had gotten this idea of fair and unfair. How can someone call a line crooked if he has no idea of a straight line? What was he comparing these things with that disturbed him so much that he called it unfair? As simple and as profound as these questions and arguments are, they were completely new to me. He knew, and I am glad I was told, that there was something else directing our behavior and shaping our view of right and wrong, just and unjust.

It is my hope that this book will appeal to those familiar with Lewis and those that know nothing about him. I am certain of one thing: if Lewis is read with an open mind, those that believe will find assurance in his words, those that do not believe will be given pause, and those who are on the fence will come down on one side or the other.

I must warn the reader that you will quickly realize, if you haven't already, that I am not a trained theologian, apologist, Bible scholar, or any other kind of scholar. If there is a justification for someone so unlearned in writing such a book, I can only offer the same reason Lewis offered when admitting he was an amateur. In his introductory to *Reflections on the Psalms*, Lewis admitted he was no expert in the field he was writing about but added that often the novice can help more than the expert. Sometimes, the expert does not see what is bothering the student because the master has overcome those problems long ago. He thinks the student should be worried about something completely different. Here is hoping a fellow student can help.

My goal is to offer the reader the books and thoughts in Lewis's writings that helped me the most—the things that made me question long-held views and appreciate new ones. But most importantly, his arguments confirmed the essence of the Gospel I had believed since I could remember. What was helpful to me may not be helpful to you. You may disagree with my interpretation of what is here. However, I urge you to read Lewis's words for yourself. He writes brilliant, eloquent prose. You draw your own conclusions.

Lewis was a man who seldom read a newspaper but whose opinions and writings today are more current and practical than the daily news—someone who could have cared less about politics yet his writings predicted, with astounding accuracy, the rise of political correctness. He also predicted the detrimental effect of the idea of the existence of absolute truth being removed from the classroom. His theology is classic, yet he was not a trained theologian. One can only surmise that his writings, some over eighty years old, are still so relevant because they were grounded in eternal truths, which are best revealed in Christian faith. As he wrote in *The Four Loves*, "What is not eternal is eternally out of date." Lewis is much more current than your last tweet or Facebook post.

Lewis was a writer who wrote so unassumingly that when he finished one book, he would turn the papers over and write another book on the blank sheets of the first book. Most of his original transcripts were burned. He wrote with an ink pen that required an inkwell to refill. He could only write four or five words at a time before refilling his pen. He was said to write an almost-perfect prose on the first try. Two-thirds of the royalties from his books went to widows and orphans through a foundation he established after his works became popular.

Most importantly, this book is not written to glorify C. S. Lewis but to point to the One he wrote about. At the end of his autobiography, *Surprised by Joy*, Lewis says if you are lost in the woods, a signpost pointing the direction home is an important thing. After you see it, you don't stop and stare at the other signs. We use the other signs to help us on our way, and we give thanks to the One who put them there. I give thanks to the *one* who gave C. S. Lewis the gifts to write as he did and leave the signposts.

"The Kilns" Lewis's home near Oxford for over 30 years.

CHAPTER 1
The Loss of Faith and Its Return

Clive Staples "Jack" Lewis was born in Belfast, Ireland (now Northern Ireland) on November 28, 1898. His father, Albert, was a lawyer. His mother, Flora, was a college graduate with degrees in mathematics and logic. He had a brother, Warren (Warnie), three years his elder. Lewis's mother was the stable influence in his life. His father was prone to more emotional states, which embarrassed Lewis.

In a series of rapid events Lewis's life was quickly changed from one of security and nurture to uncertainty and cruelty. At the age of nine, Lewis's mother died a painful death due to cancer. Her surgery was done at home, as it so often was in those days. He was told to pray in faith for her recovery, which he did. Her recovery did not occur. His father's natural emotionalism became worse and an even bigger embarrassment for the young Lewis.

His father, at a loss as how to deal with his wife's death and his two young sons, sent Lewis to England to boarding school with his brother. His mother's death occurred on August 23; he was in school at Wynyard in Watford, England less than thirty days later. Lewis's father lost his father, wife, and brother in rapid order, only adding to his grief and confusion.

One can only imagine the insecurity a bright nine-year-old would feel given these drastic changes. To make the situation even worse, the first school he attended at Watford after his mother's death was run by a headmaster who was later committed to an insane asylum. Lewis described this time at Wynyard in his autobiography, *Surprised by Joy*. It was punctuated by cruelty and homesickness.

Between 1908 and 1913, he attended three different schools until 1914 when he went to live with a personal tutor, W. T. Kirkpatrick. He was known by the Lewis family as the Great Knock. The Great Knock was a former headmaster of a school Lewis's father had attended and was a friend of the family.

Lewis lived with Kirkpatrick and his wife in Surrey, England for two years. He was probably the greatest single influence on Lewis's life for good and ill. He prepared Lewis for his examinations needed to enter Oxford. He was also an atheist.

Lewis said of Kirkpatrick that he was consumed by logical speech. No casual conversation or idle talk was tolerated. In Lewis's view, Kirkpatrick's communication was used only to transmit useful information. I can imagine a character like Dr. Spock in *Star Trek*.

However, the Great Knock laid the foundation in classic literature that helped make Lewis one of the greatest scholars and writers of the twentieth century. Ironically, his nonbelieving teacher also showed him the value of concise and probing questioning, which honed his logic, critical thinking, writing, and later, his apologetics. All this was done by an unwitting atheist. Lewis described his first meeting with Kirkpatrick in his autobiography, *Surprised by Joy*. It was funny and revealed the sort of teaching method Kirkpatrick used, a method Lewis adopted later. Despite the Great Knock's atheism, Lewis said in later life about Kirkpatrick, "My debt to him is great, my reverence to this day undiminished."

It is no wonder that at this impressionable age, Kirkpatrick helped push Lewis along his road to becoming an avowed and outspoken atheist. Little did the Great Knock know he was also preparing Lewis for the "greatest knock" of all by the God of all creation.

There were other unusual things that moved Lewis toward writing and scholarship—for instance, his thumbs. Lewis and his brother had a congenital oddity shared with their father. The upper joint in their thumbs would not bend. Lewis himself said it made him clumsy at almost any task, except writing. ("I could, at least hold a pencil.") His physical clumsiness was the reason he never drove a car. He failed the driving test four times.

After a short time with Lewis as his student, Kirkpatrick told Lewis's father that his son had little talent for anything else other than as a writer or scholar. He would become one of the best of both.

As you might assume, Lewis was a voracious reader. His home as a child was full of books, and he said he was denied nothing he wanted to read. Consequently, books were another of the ways—not as mysterious as nonbelieving teachers and congenital oddities—the Lord worked on Lewis. Christian authors, whom he enjoyed reading most, always seemed to be just around the corner.

One of the first authors that had significant influence on Lewis was George McDonald. In 1916, Lewis read his book *Phantasies.* He said after reading the book, he "knew he had crossed a great frontier." He also wrote that it "baptized" his imagination. Lewis said later that there was almost nothing he wrote in which he did not quote McDonald, a preacher and theologian. This will be a common recurrence in Lewis's later conversion. The authors he liked best had that "bee in their bonnet"; almost all of them were Christians.

In 1917, Lewis began his studies at the University College, Oxford. Except for his time in the service during World War I, Oxford would be his professional home until he accepted a professorship at Cambridge University in 1955.

Less than a full term into the University College in 1917, Lewis was called into the army. He was commissioned a second lieutenant in the Somerset Light Infantry. He arrived in France on his nineteenth birthday, November 29, 1917. He was wounded at Mt. Berne near Lille, France in April 1918.

Before being wounded, while sick with trench fever, he read for the first time a volume of essays by G. K. Chesterton. He had never heard of Chesterton and was surprised he liked him particularly given Lewis's own pessimism and atheism. In *Surprised by Joy,* Lewis admitted that he was ignorant about what was happening to him by reading the works of these two authors, Chesterton and MacDonald. He soon learned that he could not be too careful about what he read, especially if he wanted to remain an atheist. God, he found out, was very "unscrupulous."

Although Lewis said he met many men and read authors that were believers in the First World War, his pessimism surely grew and hardened. His descriptions of "horribly smashed men still moving like half-crushed beetles, the sitting or half standing corpses," his kindly sergeant who he thought was killed by the same shell that wounded him, would have certainly made him rebel at the concept of a loving, merciful God.

Before Lewis left for France and the war, he became friends with a young soldier E. F. C. "Paddy" Moore. They made a promise to each other that if either was killed, the survivor would pledge to take care of the other's parent. Paddy's mother was divorced and Lewis's father a widower. Paddy was killed in action. Lewis fulfilled his pledge and cared for Moore's mother until her death in 1951.

After returning to Oxford, he excelled as a student and won first in honor moderations in 1920, first in the Greats (classics and philosophy) in 1922, and first in English language and literature in 1923. He became a tutor at the University College in 1924. In 1925, much to the relief of Lewis and his father, he was elected Fellow in English Language and Literature at the Magdalen College, Oxford. Despite his mother having a degree in mathematics, Lewis was terrible in math. He failed the math part of the entrance exam for Oxford twice. It was only through an exemption given to returning soldiers of the First World War to forgo the math exam that allowed Lewis's acceptance at Oxford.

Lewis, his father, and Kirkpatrick all agreed he would never have passed the math hurdle without the exemption and, consequently, never been an Oxford professor.

Many things happened to Lewis after the war that helped his return to faith and ultimately Christianity. Along with the books he read, he was influenced by several friends. The most influential was Owen Barfield.

Owen Barfield was almost exactly the same age as Lewis. He was born on November 9, 1898, just twenty days before Lewis. They met at Oxford in 1919. Almost immediately, they started what Lewis called "The Great War," an intellectual debate about the meaning of life. When they first met, Lewis told Barfield he was an "atheist who did not accept God."

However, Lewis admitted in the first battle of the war Barfield quickly refuted what Lewis described as his "chronological snobbery." The term means the assumption that things that are no longer practiced or believed had been proven false. Lewis was made to understand by Barfield that one must ask obvious questions. Was it ever refuted (and if so, by whom, where, and how conclusively), or did it merely die away as fashions do? Had Lewis discounted belief in God because God had been proven not to exist, or had his belief in him just gone out of fashion? In *Surprised by Joy*, Lewis also concluded he had given up faith not because it had been proven wrong but because he had stopped believing.

How many things do we accept today without question? How many things have we stopped doing because we think we don't have to do them anymore or perhaps we believe they have been proven to be false or discredited? Are we like children doing things simply because everybody else does it or not doing them simply because no one else does? Perhaps "chronological snobbery" was an early form of political correctness.

Barfield finally showed him that there was something that existed outside our senses. Barfield also helped Lewis to see that the "Absolute" (God) Lewis and most people understood was one that was impersonal. It was a religion that costs nothing. We could talk about this mysterious God, but there was no danger of "It" (God) doing anything. It was somewhere else and would never come here.

Lewis began to see that the God of the universe, as he wrote in *Miracles*, prefers one thing over the other and one action over another.

Lewis later dedicated *The Lion, the Witch and the Wardrobe* to Barfield's daughter, Lucy. Lucy is also one of the children's name in the story. He also dedicated *The Voyage of the Dawn Trader* to Barfield's son, Geoffrey.

Another and more well-known friend of Lewis who helped in his journey back to faith was J. R. R. Tolkien. Tolkien was also an unlikely source of help.

In *Surprised by Joy*, Lewis said that before he got to Oxford, he had been taught never to trust a papist (Roman Catholic). At Oxford, he was told never to trust a philologist (a person who studies ancient words). Friendship with Tolkien marked a breakdown of two prejudices. Tolkien was both a Catholic and a scholar of ancient words.

Those that are familiar with the works of Tolkien need not be reminded of his great epics, *The Hobbit* and *The Lord of the Rings*. His help to Lewis, however, was simple and obvious and consequently overlooked many times.

As an atheist, Lewis assumed the Gospels and the story of Jesus were just another myth like the ones Lewis had loved as a child. The Gospel of Christ was just like the myths of the "dying god" who had given new life to man, the idea that had helped spark his longing for joy. Tolkien argued these myths were a God-given foretaste of the joy Christ held and the Gospels told. He also pointed out that Lewis only rejected the joy of the reality of Christ exactly because it was *not a myth. It was true!* The story in the Gospels, consequently, did not hold the same mystery and appeal as the stories of his childhood. Tolkien made Lewis see that with the life of Christ, myth had become reality. An infinite God had entered finite human history. All the other myths were but glimpses of God's plan he had given to other people at different times.

After studying the Gospels in their entirety, Lewis also realized that the Gospels were not written as myths. Lewis, of all people, knew what a myth looked, sounded, and felt like. The Gospels, he concluded, were not a myth. For instance, when Christ was depicted as drawing in the dust in the Gospel of John, that event—in Lewis' opinion—really happened. Lewis contended that that recorded act would have been completely out of place in a myth.

Other friends began to appear who had that "bee in their bonnet." One was Neville Coghill. Lewis met him in his first class in English school at Oxford. According to Lewis, Coghill's first remarks made him stand out above all the others. Lewis was soon shocked to learn he, who was a Christian and the most intelligent and best-informed in the class, was also a "thoroughgoing" supernaturalist. There were other traits that he liked about Coghill but found archaic—chivalry, honor, courtesy, freedom, and *gentillesse*. Lewis imagined he was the type who would fight a duel. His traits were out of date. (To prove the point, *gentillesse* always activates my spell-check. Perhaps it is a word out of fashion. It means kindness.)

Then, in addition to the books and the people he liked most turning against his world view, "something far more alarming" happened to Lewis. One of the most devout atheists he knew walked into his room at the Magdalen College, Oxford and said that it appeared that the stories about a dying god really happened once.

The final events of Lewis's conversion to theism are detailed in the chapter "Checkmate" in his autobiography, *Surprised by Joy*. Anyone can read and understand the last paragraph of that chapter, where Lewis describes the approach of the one he wanted no part of. He sums up the encounter and God's pursuit when he describes how he became the most disappointed convert in all of England. Lewis wondered how one could properly adore a God that would take a convert on such terms. At least, the prodigal freely returned home. Lewis called it "divine humility." He summed up his conversion this way. What God compels us to do finally liberates us. "The hardness of God is kinder than the softness of men, and his compulsion is our liberation."

This initial conversion was to theism (the belief in a god). His friends continued to work on Lewis; and on September 19, 1931, Tolkien and Hugo Dyson, who were visiting Lewis for dinner, stayed late into the night and resolved many doctrines of the faith for him. Soon after, Lewis wrote to another friend, Arthur Greeves, that he had passed on from being a theist to believing in Christ.

A wise man once told me that the difference between what you are now and the person you will be in the future will be determined in great part by the people you meet and the books you read. That is certainly true in Lewis's case and my own. His search for joy and truth was helped by friends and authors from the past. As was mine.

Lewis's faith gave rise to his prolific professional work. We will be looking at part of the prodigious literary and the apologetic works that he left to the world and affected my notion of reality.

The "New Building" at Magdalen College Oxford.
Where Lewis tutored and the "Inklings" met on Thursdays

CHAPTER 2
Faith Shows Its Fruit

The first conversion of Lewis, as described in *Surprised by Joy*, was to theism alone. Lewis did not accept Christ as Savior until two years later. He did, however, begin attending church at his local parish. On a trip to the national zoo with his brother, he simply recorded in the last chapter of *Surprised by Joy* that when he began the trip, he did not believe Jesus was the Son of God. When they arrived at the zoo, he believed. Not exactly an earth-shattering experience. I believe Lewis would have found the term "born-again Christian" a puzzling or at least a redundant term. Becoming a new creature in Christ is the whole of Christianity. It is not a special designation.

If one looks at the work Lewis produced after his conversion, you can see what a tremendous effect Christianity had on him as a writer. He published *The Pilgrims Regress: An Allegorical Apology for Christianity, Reason and Romanticism.* The most significant thing about this book was that Lewis dropped the pseudonym of Clive Hamilton (his first name, Clive, and his mother's maiden name, Hamilton). He would write one other book twenty-seven years later, using the pseudonym N. W. Clerk, titled *A Grief Observed.* It is the story of the death of his wife and his ensuing grief.

Between 1933 and 1940, he also published five other works. The book I read of the five that meant most to me was *The Problem of Pain* in 1940—to be more exact, the introductory to the book. It describes Lewis's argument as to why he had been an atheist. It is an eloquent and concise explanation for his lack of faith. It centered mostly on viewing the universe from the most pessimistic of all views.

After describing the immenseness of the universe—that it is completely dark and unimaginably cold and that there is little reason to believe any of the other bodies in space contain any life like ours—and even if all the planets were inhabited with perfectly happy creatures, it would appear that happiness was simply a by-product of the power that created the universe.

Then, Lewis went on to ask what life was like while it lasted. It is started in pain, and it dies in pain and has the unfortunate ability to see all this happening to itself.

After even more pessimistic pronouncements, he then posed one question that had never occurred to him before. He wondered how a world so constructed could ever have been credited to a loving God. He said it is mere nonsense to put pain among the discoveries of science. Then, he asked the reader to contemplate for five minutes about a world without chloroform and how mankind could attribute the creation of this cruel world to a merciful God.

I had never thought of that. What a way to look at faith in relationship to the cruelty of the world. I would suggest to anyone who is interested in reading more of Lewis to read the introductory or preface of any of his books, and you will learn more there than reading entire books of other authors.

Other books written between 1933 and 1940 were *The Allegory of Love: A Study in Medieval Tradition* in 1936; *Out the Silent Planet*, the first in a space trilogy, in 1938; and *The Personal Heresy: A Controversy* with E. M. W. Tillyard and *Rehabilitations and Other Essays*, both in 1939.

At this time, Lewis also began to do lectures for the military. England was now at war with the greatest physical threat ever presented to England and Christian culture.

The Inklings

Lewis enjoyed nothing more than the company of friends and freewheeling discussions of religion, literature, philosophy, and nonsense. Beginning in the early 1930s, Lewis met with a group of friends in his rooms at the Magdalen College, usually on Thursday nights. The last recorded meeting that appeared in Warren Lewis's diary was on October 20, 1949. Lewis's comment about loving Christian friends around a fire was no doubt a result of his fondness for this group of friends. The group would also meet on Tuesdays at a local pub, usually The Eagle and the Child or, as they called it, the Bird and the Baby. The group became something of local lore. In fact, there is a reference to the group meeting at the pub in a detective novel written in the late '40s. The character was made to say, "It must be Tuesday—there is Lewis going into the Bird."

The members of the group varied, and the gatherings were informal. They called themselves the "Inklings." The meetings, though casual in nature, were dramatic in their results. The members would use this time to read what each had been writing and accept praise, encouragement, and criticism—the latter being severe at times— from the others. Little did they know, especially Lewis and Tolkien, that what was read to their friends would later generate billions of dollars in the sales of books and movies of their "children stories." The gross revenue from movies generated from Lewis's Narnia series and Tolkien's The Hobbit and The Lord of the Rings trilogy have topped over 2.5 billion dollars worldwide. This amount, of course, does not include all the money the Lewis and Tolkien books produced and still continue to generate.

The idea that these classic bestsellers were first read to each other by the authors seems incredible. The genesis of Lewis's and Tolkien's epics stemmed from the regret by the two that since no one was writing the kinds of books they liked, they determined to write them themselves. Their success also reinforces the notion that any literary work based on a true picture of reality (good versus evil) and the struggles that result from that picture of truth has a universal attraction. In fact, Lewis and Tolkien encouraged each other with their efforts, particularly with the Lord of the Rings and The Chronicles of Narnia series. There are indications that Lewis was more encouraging to Tolkien than the other way around and in fact prodded Tolkien to complete the works when he was about to give up. In a letter to a friend in 1959, Lewis said of Tolkien that no one could ever influence Tolkien. When they listened to his work, encouragement was the only thing that helped. His reaction to criticism was either to ignore it or start the work all over.

Lewis also first read to the Inklings *The Problem of Pain*, *Miracles*, and *The Screwtape Letters*.

In a memoir of his brother after his death, Warren Lewis gave an account of an Inkling meeting from his diary. Warren recorded in his diary of 1946 "a vintage year." Warnie described hearing Tolkien reading *The Hobbit* among other serious and comical performances. His diary records in November that Roy Campbell read them his translations of a couple of Spanish poems, and John Wain won a bet by reading a chapter of Irene Iddesleigh without a smile. Warren went on to say that when no one had anything to read, the evenings were passed in laughter.

Those most mentioned as attendees were Owen Barfield; J. A. W. Bennett; Lord David Cecil; Neville Coghill; Hugo Dyson; Adam Fox; Roger Lance Lyn Green; Robert Havard; C. S. Lewis; Warren Lewis; J. R. R. Tolkien and Christopher Tolkien, the former's son; and Charles Williams, an accomplished author in his own right. Lewis considered Williams one of the most talented authors and lecturers of his time. William's premature and sudden death in 1945 was a great shock to Lewis.

Marriage, Death, and Legacy

One of the most time-consuming parts of Lewis's daily life was answering mail from admirers. As his fame as a writer and apologist grew, so did his correspondence. He felt an obligation to respond to every inquiry. His brother, Warren, helped when the volume became overwhelming. One lady from Savannah, Georgia corresponded so much that a book of his replies to her letters was published after his death. *Letters to an American Lady* was published in 1967.

In 1950, Lewis began to correspond with a lady in America, Joy Davidman Gresham. She and her husband at the time were both fans of Lewis. Joy was born a Jew. Later she became a communist-atheist. She became a Christian partly due to Lewis's books. The Gresham's marriage was troubled. He was an alcoholic and a womanizer. They had two children, both boys. In 1953, Joy and her boys came to England. She was a writer herself. She had also won several poetry awards.

Lewis admired her literary talents and became friends when she came to England to meet him. She stayed for some time, working on a book. Joy's visa ran out while she was in London and would not be renewed by the British government. By then, she was divorced from Gresham.

Lewis, in order to allow her to remain in England, offered to marry her in a civil ceremony. A few months after their marriage, Joy was diagnosed with an advanced cancer. Lewis, giving in to his real feelings for her, agreed to marry her in a religious ceremony. He married Joy in a civil service on April 1956. He married her in an Anglican ceremony on January 1957 while Joy was in the hospital with what they thought to be a terminal cancer.

The Anglican union was not without complications. Since she was divorced, the Church of England would not perform the ceremony. Lewis convinced an Anglican priest to do the ceremony in Joy's hospital room.

The prognosis of Joy's health was dire. The doctors gave her only months at best to live. Lewis asked this same priest to pray for her recovery. Lewis also prayed that God would transfer her disease to him (a prayer of substitution). Soon, the bone in her leg that was ravaged by the cancer was made whole. Lewis suddenly experienced a loss of bone density, which became very painful.

After his marriage to Joy, he told a friend that he never expected to be married so late in life and enjoy the companionship he had missed earlier. Joy's recovery allowed Lewis a few years of happiness he never expected. Joy's cancer recurred, and she died on June 13, 1960.

Lewis wrote a book expressing his grief about his wife's death. It is titled *A Grief Observed*. The first edition was written by Lewis under a pseudonym, N. W. Clerk (a part of a term used for assistants who do research for Oxford Dons that loosely translates as "I know not which clerk did it."). His mask was quickly removed, and he then published it with his name attached. It is a classic for the bereaved to read.

There was also a movie and a play produced that tells this love story. It is called "Shadowlands."

Between 1950 when he received his first letter from Joy to his death in 1963, Lewis published some of his greatest works. He also changed his employment after twenty-five years from Oxford to Cambridge.

If you are old enough to remember where you were when John F. Kennedy was assassinated, you will remember where you were when C. S. Lewis died. John F. Kennedy was killed at noon (CST) in Dallas, Texas on Friday, November 22, 1963. C. S. Lewis died at his home in Oxford, England, almost exactly at the same time. It was late afternoon in England.

I can remember Kennedy's death. I was in a Georgia history class in Waycross, Georgia. I was thirteen years old. At the age of eleven, I had written President Kennedy about a famine in Africa. I got a reply from George McGovern, his agricultural secretary, explaining the administration's stance on the subject. My mother delivered it to me at Isabella Street School so I could read it to the class. This was, so it seemed to me at the time, a big deal in 1961 in Waycross, Georgia.

When JFK was killed two years later, I was very attentive and watched the tragedy unfold over and over again on television. Little did I know the one whose writings helped my view of the world much more died at the same time. Of course, Lewis's obituary was completely overshadowed by the death of Kennedy. I would submit his legacy may prove to be more important than the president's. Aldous Huxley, author of *Brave New World,* also died that day.

The next chapter details the origin of *Mere Christianity,* the book that changed my view of my faith and made me face what I professed to believe as a Christian.

BBC Studio where Lewis's gave the "Broadcast Talks"
that became the book "Mere Chritianity."

CHAPTER 3

The Broadcast Talks and Mere Christianity

World War II began for England on September 1, 1939 when Germany invaded Poland. By 1941, when Lewis was asked to do a series of radio broadcasts by the BBC, London was enduring bombing from the most maniacal of men bent on world domination. Yet in spite of the turmoil, Lewis was asked to explain to the British public "what Christians believe." There were over twenty broadcasts, which began in 1942. Between 1942 and 1944, there were three small books published that comprised the "talks." They were in order of publication: *Broadcast Talks*, *Christian Behavior*, and *Beyond Personality*. Ten years later these three booklets became the book, *Mere Christianity*.

During the war, his voice on the radio became the second most popular next to Churchill's. In fact, after the war, Lewis was offered a medal by Churchill for his work during the war. Lewis also spent time giving talks to members of the British military all over England. He refused the medal because he thought it would compromise his impartiality with those reading his apologetic work.

Lewis was faced with a problem in preparing the talks. How does one explain and defend the faith as Lewis saw and believed it to many who did not believe in God nor accept the authority of scripture or the authority or traditions of the church? He had to find a common starting point with which anyone could agree and, at the same time, had no direct relationship to religion.

Lewis chose to use the existence of a universal moral law as proof of a lawmaker and a lawgiver. He called this moral law the "law of nature." He, for instance, asked the listener to try to find a place where people were rewarded for deserting in battle or where someone was praised for double-crossing all his friends. He felt there was not such a country. Some might as well try to find a place where one plus one made three. These notions have been common to different civilizations, religions, and cultures through all of history.

He also showed how this real moral law is "always pressing on us." He noted that we can always find excuses for our bad behavior, but we give ourselves credit for our good behavior.

Lewis concluded the chapter on "The Law of Human Nature" by saying the two things that are obvious about human behavior is that we all know we ought to behave in a certain way and that we don't do it. These facts in Lewis's mind show we are all sinners in need of a savior.

All one has to do is look at six thousand years of recorded history of mankind to confirm his conclusion. There is no greater empirical evidence of that reality that we all behave badly. And we will continue to do it. We ignore this fact at our peril.

Lewis also noted that we learn more about God through the moral law he has given us than by looking at the world he has created, just as we can learn more about a man from what he says than by looking at something he has built. The conclusions Lewis drew from that analogy were spot-on. Obviously, he concluded that the "force" behind the moral law must be very interested in right conduct, and we continually go against his desires.

Theologians and scholars have tried to complicate the message of the Gospel. Lewis was trying to explain the simple question the Christian faith answers. We are sinners in need of a savior. He did it by making them face the reality of sin. He said he was merely trying to make people understand the questions Christianity is supposed to answer. We may not agree with his analysis or the claims of Christianity, but in Lewis's opinion, there is no doubt that the recognition of one being a sinner is the first step in Lewis's version of Christianity.

That is a far cry from those today who claim the first step is to recognize your greatness within and turn it into prosperity for yourself. Read the chapter in *Mere Christianity* titled "We Have Cause to Be Uneasy." It portrays the state of our existence and the reason and need for our faith. The message of Christianity is simple. Christianity, according to Lewis, offers no help for people who do not believe they have done anything wrong and do not need to be forgiven.

One of the great things about *Mere Christianity* is that each chapter stands on its own. You can pick the book up and turn to any chapter, read it, and understand Lewis's point. Lewis said as much in the chapter "Time and Beyond." He said it is a very silly idea that in reading a book you must never skip. He said if you find this chapter of no use skip it. The important thing about that advice is that you can use it with almost every chapter of Lewis's apologetic writing. If you are reading something that does not interest you skip it and find something that does.

The chapters you like will help you on their own. The chapter he asked us to skip if needed is about the idea of God attending to billions of prayers at the same time. That is something I never worried about. If God can raise a man from the dead, why can't he hear billions of prayers at the same time? Lewis's explanation is plausible.

Mere Christianity is helpful as a reference for no other reason. It is divided into four books, each of which are wonderful explanations of the basic tenants of our faith and their application. First, he established the need for our faith in *Right and Wrong as a Clue to the Meaning of the Universe*, the first of the books that make up *Mere Christianity*. It is an argument, as expressed earlier, that points to a moral law that we did not make up but yet we all feel pressing on us.

In book two, *What Christians Believe*, Lewis compares different religions and different conceptions of God, the meaning of the Crucifixion, and how Christianity is spread. He believed, in his experience, that Christianity is the religion that most nearly explains the human condition. Book three, *Christian Behavior*, discussed the major parts of the Christian life that we encounter every day. And finally, book four, *Beyond Personality or First Steps in the Doctrine of the Trinity*, Lewis showed what becoming a new creature was like. He also showed us that Christ had come not to give us more good advice but to make something new of us. He even changed our motives for the things we do. In the final page of *Mere Christianity*, Lewis stated that our true personality will not be shown until we give it up to Christ. Sameness is to be found in the *natural* men, not among those who surrender to Christ. The worst of us, according to Lewis, are all alike and very much monotonous to experience. It is the saints that are so delightfully different.

Just as Jack Nicolaus said he looked at the basics, so should we when our faith lags. *Mere Christianity* is a great tool for the nonbeliever, the beginner, and the experienced Christian who finds something wrong with his faith.

After Lewis argued the existence of a righteous and holy God whose Law we continually break, he presented the chapter "The Shocking Alternative." It is the chapter in *Mere Christianity* I like most. It is the chapter that explains and defends some of the most often asked questions about Christianity. It does not offer proof, but it does give concise and logical argument that begs us to answer the most important of all questions—the deity of Christ. As you will see, "The Shocking Alternative" offers no halfway house when one confronts the claims of Jesus.

The Shocking Alternative

In this chapter of *Mere Christianity*, Lewis addressed questions that had always puzzled me. He offered reasonable, though not sure, patented answers to those questions. Faith is always required, but logical explanations help immensely. I don't suppose there are more difficult questions posed and explained in fewer words here than almost anywhere in any other apologetic work by any other author.

For instance, why would an all-powerful God allow a "dark power" to become the "prince of the world"? Lewis explains that because God allowed "free will," evil was made possible. Why, Lewis then asks, did he give us free will? The answer is simple, direct, and profound. If we had no choice but to love, whatever love we somehow showed would be meaningless. Behaving like machines is not what God desires. God wants us to freely love him. The happiness God wants for us is the joy of being freely united with him. That type of love requires all parties to be free.

If we are concerned about the price we pay for free will, Lewis said don't worry. The reward is worth the cost.

This explanation of evil and the worth of free will to God may have been a tough sell to his fellow citizens who were suffering at the hands of free will running amok. Nevertheless, the "talks" were very popular. This common-sense explanation is still popular to many today.

The fall of man is also tackled by Lewis. Once again, his explanation is admittedly a reasonable and a traditional guess. But once again, it is true to life. When most of us fall, it is when we put ourselves first. I know the biggest mistakes I have made in my life were when I was thinking of myself, not others. According to Lewis, we are all trying to act as if we created ourselves. We fall in the same way as Satan—wanting to be God.

The key to history, according to Lewis, is that Satan has us running on the wrong power. He pointed out that we have the best and brightest spending time and money to make heaven on earth and ultimately, it all fails. We are continually at odds with each other about our individual self-interests. One of the successes of our republic is that the founders recognized this truth of human nature—hence, three branches of government. The job is to make sure one branch nor one person ever accumulates too much power.

The final point made in "The Shocking Alternative" is what has been called the *trilemma*. This is what Lewis suggested about the deity of Jesus and how we can only explain it in one of three ways.

In God's response to man's fall, Lewis outlined the biblical story in his usual way—with a brilliant summation of the Old Testament. According to Lewis, it even took God several centuries to make the Jews understand that there was only one God and that he cared about the way one acts.

Then, Lewis said, comes the real shock. These Jews produced a man that acted as if he were God. He boasted that he had always existed. He said he would come back to judge the world. He even said he could forgive sins.

The most astounding claim, the forgiveness of sin, has been heard so often that we don't understand the implication anymore. Lewis paints a comical picture of a man himself uninjured and forgiving injuries done to other people by others. Jim steps on Joe's toe, and I forgive Jim for the act "without consulting" Joe. If someone stole your money and I acted as if I had the power to forgive your thief, you would think I was stupid. If Jesus is not God, his acts of forgiveness are simply 'asinine fatuity' (stupidity). Jesus responds as if he was the person who was hurt most by the sins of others. In Lewis's opinion, these acts of Jesus's forgiveness of sin only made sense if Jesus was the God whose law had been broken and whose Love was wounded with each sin.

Lewis said he was trying to stop a common misunderstanding about Jesus. Lewis believed that the popular conception of Jesus was that he was a great moral teacher, but also that he was not God. It is also a convenient excuse for not giving complete due to the lordship of Christ. Lewis concluded that he couldn't be just a great moral teacher. A moral teacher would not act as if he were God unless he really were God. Lewis concluded Jesus was either a Liar, Lunatic, or Lord. And Lewis added, what good is one more great moral teacher? We have never been lacking in moral teachers. Even if he is the best moral teacher, that would only make it less likely we would follow his teaching.

There you have it. Lewis did not prove Jesus is Lord; he simply pointed out that there is no middle ground in what one can believe about him. This chapter did more for my understanding of the importance and uniqueness of Christ as Savior than anything I had previously read.

In other books, Lewis used even more detailed examples of this idea of all or nothing as to how we react to the claims of Jesus. He pointed out that if one were to ask any one of the other religious leaders of history—from Buddha to Mohammed to Confucius—if they were God, the reply would be a very clear no. Lewis suggested that Mohammed would reply *no* after he had torn his clothing and then severed your head for even asking the question. It is true. No other religion suggests its leader is God incarnate. Lewis expressed this view in the essay "What Are We to Make of Jesus Christ" found in the book *God in the Dock.* Lewis backed up this view expressed in the trilemma by saying there were only three responses to Jesus recorded in the scriptures: hatred, terror, and adoration. No one ever showed "mild approval." There may be an argument that we and the current church have achieved a mild approval of Christ.

I have found through the years of discussing *Mere Christianity* with many people that their main complaint is that it is too difficult to understand. I believe the opposite is true. Lewis uses very understandable simple analogies. One thing I have learned reading a lot of Lewis's writings is that I am an auditory learner. I learn better by listening rather than reading. For what it is worth, I read passages aloud that I do not grasp the first time. It helps me a great deal.

In the last two books of *Mere Christianity, Christian Behavior* and *Beyond Personality*, very practical words are given on everything from sexual morality and Christian marriage to charity, hope, and faith. Some of the advice Lewis gives, written nearly seventy-five years ago, may seem out of date. However, Lewis—I believe once again—gets the biblical belief right. What you or the culture believes is irrelevant to Lewis.

Some of the most useful ideas in the last two "books" of *Mere Christianity* I have recorded in the next two chapters of this book (books three and four of *Mere Christianity*). I will also give a brief explanation of what I see as Lewis's main idea in the chapter. I hope their inclusion will make you want to read more about his explanations and thoughts on various subjects.

Book 3 of Mere Christianity—Christian Behavior

Chapter 1—"Three Parts of Morality." In this chapter, Lewis compares the three parts of morality addressed by Christian thought (fair play, harmony with others, and making the individual better inside).

Chapter 2—"The Cardinal Virtues." Here, Lewis reviews and explains the "important" virtues we seldom hear about today: prudence, temperance, justice, and fortitude. Note how the meaning of these words (with the exception of fortitude) have changed. All other virtues *hinge* on these four: common sense, moderation, fairness, and courage.

Chapter 3—"Social Morality." Lewis maintains that Christianity cannot give us a program of how a government ought to work. We all want to pick and choose the bits of the doctrine we like best. And he says Christ did not come to preach a "new morality."

Chapter 4—"Morality and Psychoanalysis." Lewis discusses the moral choices of different types of people.

Chapter 5—"Sexual Morality." Lewis reviews the most uncompromising and least liked of all the Christian virtues—chastity.

Chapter 6—"Christian Marriage." Although he was not married at the time he wrote it, he expressed this balanced view of what Christians believe about marriage.

Chapter 7—"Forgiveness." Here, we are shown the person we know that we always forgive.

Chapter 8—"The Great Sin." Lewis shows us that this is where the center of Christian morals lies. The word *conceited* here is used as pride. Pride was the downfall of Satan and Adam and the cause of our personal failure. Lewis shows how to determine if one is prideful.

Chapter 9—"Charity." Lewis talks about how the meaning of the word charity has changed. It is pure Christian "love," not only giving to the poor. He gives a very practical tip on how to learn to like those you don't like. Pretend as you do like them. This is a good pretense.

Chapter 10—"Hope." You may be surprised what Lewis says about hope. Hope is always looking forward to the world beyond. He says Christians have become ineffectual because they have stopped talking about heaven. He contends when you take your eyes off heaven, you miss earth too. He believes that since he is not content in this world, he must be made for another world.

Chapters 11 and 12—"Faith." Lewis describes faith in two ways. In one sense, we use faith to combat our changing emotions. The second sense of faith is that what we don't see or understand now we will be shown later. We need faith to believe we will see and understand it one day.

Book 4—Beyond Personality: Or First Steps in the Doctrine of the Trinity

Chapter 1—"Making and Begetting." Lewis helps us understand the difference between us and Christ. Christ came to make us like him. He wants us to be more than a created creature. Lewis shows us once again why Jesus is much more than a moral teacher. He points out that Christianity is much more than just good advice.

Chapter 2—"The Three Personal God." This is one of the best explanations of the Trinity I have ever read. The Trinity moved us from a vague idea about God to a more certain understanding because of the life of Christ.

Chapter 3—"Time and Beyond." Lewis gives us an explanation as to how God can do more than one thing at a time. This is the chapter that Lewis says to skip if it means nothing to you.

Chapter 4—"Good Infection." Lewis shows us how we pass along the life God meant us to have. It is a sort of contagious infection.

Chapter 5—"The Obstinate Toy Soldiers." I believe Lewis would have been amused by the term "born-again Christian." I think he would see it as a redundant term. As Screwtape would have called it, "Christianity with a difference." As Lewis says, becoming a new creature is the entire essence of Christianity.

Chapter 7—"Let's Pretend." Lewis gives us a very good piece of practical advice: how pretending can help us achieve things.

Chapter 8—"Is Christianity Hard or Easy." Lewis helps us focus on the goal of the state and the church. He believes "putting on Christ" is the whole of Christianity. I think in his mind this is what we call being "born again."

Chapter 9—"Counting the Cost." Lewis shows us how coming to Christ is all or nothing. Lewis describes how coming to Christ is like going to the dentist. Dentists want to fix more than the teeth that hurt. Christ wants to fix more than what is hurting you now.

Chapter 10—"Nice People or New Men." How does one gauge the quality of one's conversion? Lewis asserts it must make some change in a person's behavior. Lewis points out, however, that being a "nice person" does not necessarily equate to being saved. In fact, it is possible that being naturally nice could be an impediment to becoming a Christian.

Chapter 11—"The New Men." Lewis shows us how giving our self away is the only way to find our true self. Lewis states that the most boring people are the tyrants of the world—they are all alike. It is the saints who have their real personality because it is Christ's.

The conciseness and clearness of the prose, the logic of the arguments, the reasonableness of the message, and the acknowledgement of what is conjecture are compelling reasons to read *Mere Christianity*. I think it will be an affirmation of what you believe. It will also make you confront directly what it is you say you believe. It will help doubt and give a second thought to those who do not believe.

Mere Christianity will help one get over changing moods about belief. Lewis said it best in the chapter on "faith" in the book. I found that having a logical defense of what I believe as a Christian helps me when my emotions change. I agree with Lewis. There are times when both Christianity and atheism appear unlikely to be true. The logic of Lewis's explanations helps us tell our feelings "where to get off."

"Screwtape"

CHAPTER 4

The Screwtape Letters

The best way to drive out the devil, if he will not yield to texts of Scripture, is to jeer and flout him, for he cannot bear scorn.
　　　　　—Martin Luther, used as part of the introduction to *The Screwtape Letters*

The Screwtape Letters was first published in 1942. In a letter to his brother, Warren, Lewis told him that he listened to a speech by Hitler the night before and said although he knew what Hitler said was untrue, his words, said with conviction, almost convinced him. The next day, he finished the letter by telling his brother that the idea of a book came to him in church. The original title was to be *As One Devil to Another.* He also said later that it was written quicker and with less pleasure than any book he had written. Looking at all virtue and goodness as evil and evil as good was, I am sure, a mentally and spiritually tiring effort. We seem to do it with ease today.

The *Letters* was an instant success. In the preface of a later edition of the book, Lewis wrote that the book had a popularity he never expected, and the criticisms he received were the kind that made him know he had made his point. In the first year of publication, the book was reprinted eight times. The first appearance of the *Letters* was in installment form in the magazine the *Guardian.*

The story is about a senior devil, Screwtape, who advises his junior tempter-in-training, Wormwood, how to trick his patient into his father's (Satan) house. The resulting chapters are an amazing picture of human temptation and behavior.

You will find a number of surprises in its pages. For instance, his definition of gluttony does not necessarily limit the sin to excess. You will learn how we keep each other from church, how the devil hates to enter into the world of logical "argument," how the devil tries to hide reality, where reality and eternity actually exist, and what we can do to protect ourselves from temptation.

In 1961, Lewis released a new edition of the book, which included a new preface along with "Screwtape Proposes a Toast" ("The Toast") at the end of the book. As usual, the new preface in this edition of the book is useful by itself. "The Toast" is very prophetic. I especially would call one's attention to Lewis's description of *envy*. It is the great sin that Screwtape is advancing so strongly and praising so richly today. Also, the devil's mention of "parity of esteem" is showing itself in "spades" today. The idea today is that we cannot point out or reward excellence or criticize failure or poor performance. It is disguised as political correctness. The lie that has been sold according to Screwtape is the notion that "I'm as good as you."

In the new preface, Lewis describes hell as a place where everyone is concerned about his own reputation and advancement and where everyone has a complaint and lives in envy, self-importance, and resentment. Sounds like we have achieved not heaven on earth but rather hell on earth. Although this book is seventy-seven years old this year (2020), it is even more useful now when applied to the unbelievable changes we are seeing today. *The Screwtape Letters* give us a guideline of what to expect and why. There is almost nothing missed in this little book. Even if you don't believe in a real devil, it is one of the most compelling and complete explanations of the human condition.

The story is set in World War II or as Lewis calls it the Second German War. The "patient" of Screwtape and his nephew, Wormwood, is young enough to serve in the military. We see two wars here—the physical one and the spiritual one. The latter is much more subtle and, in many ways, harder to fight.

Lewis's economy of words here is remarkable. More is said in this book with less words than any other I have ever read. Lewis joked in his "new preface" what he learned from a friend that met a young lady who had read *Screwtape*. When he asked why she had picked *The Screwtape Letters* to read, her reply was that to effectively show she was properly prepared for an interview, she needed to show she had read something current.

"And you chose *Screwtape?*"

"Well, of course. It was the shortest."

The first time I read this fictional account of temptation, I was astounded at how practical the ideas in the book were. In fact, I conducted a time management class for our church using a great deal of *Screwtape* as a reference.

But as usual, Lewis really does not turn the light of truth as much on the devil but rather more on us. I am confident that if we are honest, we will find ourselves somewhere in these descriptions of spiritual weaknesses.

As Lewis concludes in the new preface his motive for *The Letters* in the first place was to put a new light on mankind, not to speculate about the devil and how he operated. The beauty of Lewis's work is that it does make us see ourselves differently.

Lewis dedicated *The Screwtape Letters* to J. R. R. Tolkien. The first parts of the book were read to the Inklings in 1940 or 1941. As Lewis said in his first edition of the book, he had been surprised at the response. From all accounts, the reviews were mostly favorable. *The Screwtape Letters* was his most financially successful book to date. It helped his notoriety as well. The book was popular in the United States and was something of an introduction of him here. By 1947, Lewis was on the cover of *Time Magazine*.

In this new preface (1960), Lewis goes to some length to explain how he sees the devil. Lewis said the most common question he got about the book was whether he believed in the devil. He said he did not believe in a power equal to God and self-existent. He did, however, believe in devils. He believed they are angels who have abused their power.

He further stated that it was not part of his creed but one of his opinions, and he felt his religion would not be ruined if it were proven to be false. He felt it explained a great many things and agreed with the plain simple facts of Scripture and the tradition of Christianity. It has not been contradicted by any of the sciences. Lewis's opinion, brief and to the point, "lead[s] us not into temptation but deliver[s] us from evil." This book will help give hope to make that sacred request a reality.

In the second sentence of the original preface, Lewis goes to the essence of the work of the devil. It is to believe and act in extremes. In the book, Lewis, through the voice of Screwtape, shows how God made all the pleasures; it is the devil's job to twist them or have us go too far in their enjoyment.

Lewis suggests that the two mistakes concerning devils is to disbelieve completely or to have an unhealthy interest in them. The devils are happy with both errors. They applaud an atheist and one who has an excessive interest in devils with equal glee.

Following is a brief synopsis of each chapter of the book. This book is similar to *Mere Christianity* in that it does not have to be read in order. Each chapter stands on its own. I have made brief comments on all the chapters. The goal is to give an idea of the main subject in the chapter and to pique the interest of the reader. I am certain that there are those who will think the comments thin. I agree. It is intentional.

I have named the chapters, something Lewis did not do. I hope that will help guide those interested in reading more of what interests them.

Chapter 1—"The Urgent vs. The Important"

In the first chapter of *The Screwtape Letters*, Lewis brings two very practical aspects of our life that are usually overlooked or intentionally ignored into clear focus. One mistake we constantly make is putting the urgent first and the important second. The other mistaken notion is that we cannot defend our faith or what we say we believe with argument or logic.

Chapter 2—"Missing the Log in Our Eye"

In chapter 2, the patient has become a Christian. Screwtape, however, though threatening punishment for Wormwood, does not seem overly concerned. He quickly points out the people in church the patient does not like. Screwtape also points out that there will ultimately be a letdown in the patient's conversion.

Chapter 3—"Cultivating Domestic Strife"

One of Lewis's great gifts was a piercing insight into human nature. He shows it in great measure in this chapter, as exhibited by the patient's relationship with his mother. Screwtape offers advice that will head off any improvement in his relationship with his mother, even though he has become a Christian. He suggests that his patient's prayers for his mother be very spiritual. Don't pray for her aches and pains.

Notice how Lewis points out how people who are familiar with each other can be easily manipulated to get on each other's nerves.

Chapter 4—"Perils of Prayer"

Screwtape says the best thing to do about prayer is to keep the patient from even wanting to pray.

Chapter 5—"War is a Better Place to Die"

Screwtape warns that Wormwood should not expect much from war. People know death is a real immediate possibility.

Chapter 6—"Push Bad to the Will and Good to Fantasy"

In chapter 6, Screwtape tells Wormwood to make sure the bad habits are pushed to the will of the patient and the good habits to his fantasy.

How many times have we thought about doing a kindness for someone and not followed through? We try to make it real, but our good intention remains a fantasy. The road to hell is indeed paved with good intentions. See what Lewis says about feeling and doing.

Chapter 7—"Factions and Causes"

Screwtape considers whether the patient should be made a patriot or pacifist. Handled properly either can be useful. He points out that the important thing is making politics part of his faith.

If only Screwtape could see secular causes the church is pushing now. From "global warming" to economic boycotts of Israel to same sex marriage to the endorsement of political candidates, the church has been made political beyond recognition with causes galore.

Chapter 8—"Troughs and Peaks"

This was one of the most eye-opening chapters in the book to me. It challenged my conception of how God deals with us. Better said, it made me think about it in a different way. We can be most effective when we obey, even though we don't feel like it and may even feel abandoned. The idea of taking on the suffering of Christ is completely alien to modern Christian thought. I have suffered little for my faith. In his book *The Problem of Pain*, Lewis quotes George McDonald, "The Son of God suffered unto death not that men might not suffer, but that their sufferings might be like his."

Chapter 9—"God Made the Pleasures: Use Them with Care"

Screwtape says that the trough (depressing) periods are the best times to press the sensual temptations.

He contrasts the troughs with the peaks. He reminds his student that all pleasure, in its proper form, is good for the enemy (God). Only God makes the pleasures. Satan can only try to get the humans to misuse the pleasures.

This chapter is very enlightening about the proper and improper use of pleasure.

Chapter 10—"Keeping Up with the Joneses"

In this chapter, Screwtape is delighted to hear that the patient has made some new friends. His ideas about how to use the friends to his advantage are revealing. He explains how he can get him, the patient, to agree with the new friends' views without actually saying so. We all give silent consent to things we do not agree with.

After Screwtape gives more orders about how to manipulate the patient, he advises him to make sure he spends more money than he can afford and neglect his mother.

Chapter 12—"The Gentile Slope to Hell"

This is, in my view, the most disturbing of all the letters simply because most of us fall into this trap. It is not only the big things that move us to the "father below" but the little things as well. Whatever drives us away from the "light" is useful. When Wormwood is unable to report the great sins of the patient, Screwtape goes on to describe a number of small things that can be used to capture the patient.

Screwtape understands the disappointment of Wormwood and consoles him by revealing it is not always great sins that capture the soul. The small ones are just as good, as long as they separate the man from God.

Chapter 13—"Screwtape's Greatest Fear" (Doing What You Enjoy)

In this chapter, Screwtape is beside himself because Wormwood has let the man slip through his fingers. Wormwood's mistake was letting him enjoy two simple pleasures—reading a book and taking a walk. Pleasures and pain are the only real things that give us a grounding in reality.

As a practical matter, doing what one truly loves to do is a great defense against the devil.

Chapter 14—"Grace Sufficient for the Day"

Screwtape is displeased with the patient's lack of grand pro-nouncements about his lavish promises of perpetual virtue. He is asking only for the grace to get him through the current day.

Chapter 15—"The Present Touches Eternity"

I had never thought of the present as a "touchstone" with eter-nity. It is oddly the only place we can experience a part of eternity. It is in the present that according to Screwtape, the "enemy" wants people to think about two things: eternity and the present. Giving thanks in the present is the only thing close to eternity. Screwtape wants us to be fearful of the future or to long for the past.

Chapter 16—"Attending the Same Church"

Screwtape is displeased that the patient is attending the same church, even though he is not completely satisfied with it. He wants him to be a taster of churches and expert of sorts, not a student there to learn.

Chapter 17—"Gluttony of Delicacy"

In this letter, Screwtape suggests there is more than one kind of gluttony. He also boasts that no one ever talks about gluttony anymore. Can anyone remember ever hearing a sermon on gluttony? There is, according to Screwtape, a gluttony of delicacy, as well as excess.

Chapter 18—"What's Love Got do with It?"

In this chapter, Screwtape explains the idea the "enemy" has about marriage. You may be surprised how Screwtape advises his stu-dent to approach the situation. The enemy's (God) requirement of humans is a dilemma.

Chapter 19—"Screwtape Slips"

The problem that Screwtape has with the enemy is that he cannot determine what he is up to. He cannot imagine that he really loves the "little vermin." God's unconditional love is still hard for us to understand, and its denial and our rejection of it is one of Satan's most effective attacks.

Chapter 20—"What Attracts Is Always Changing"

Screwtape tells Wormwood that the "lowerarchy" of the bureaucracy has designed change to attract its victims.

Chapter 21—"Is Your Time Your Own"

Screwtape says the best thing to do is to make the patient believe his time and his body are his. This will add to his sense of injury if he thinks a legitimate claim to them has been denied.

Chapter 22—"Falling in Love with a Christian Woman"

Screwtape is infuriated that the patient is in love with a Christian. He becomes so agitated he loses control of himself and takes on another form. Screwtape says God is, at heart, a hedonist. Pleasure is of no use to Screwtape. All the father below can do is twist the pleasure to his advantage.

Chapter 23—"Reinventing Jesus"

Screwtape believes in order to confuse his prey, the best course is to once again use the conception of a "historical Jesus." Screwtape says this is a new Jesus that is invented every thirty years or so, which uses suppression of some parts of scripture and the exaggeration of others. He says we get them to accept the expert's guessing and also get them to call them brilliant for the discovery.

Chapter 24—"Humility and Secret Societies"

Screwtape is now infuriated not only at the Christian girl but even more now since she is helping increase his circle of Christian friends. Screwtape suggests that it may be impossible "to remove spirituality from his life," so "We must corrupt it." Screwtape suggests making him proud of his Christianity and take caution to never let him ask if he really has anything to be proud of.

Chapter 25—"Christianity with a Difference"

I suspect this may be the clearest picture of the current "church" any current critic has suggested. Every church today seems to need a plan or program that sets them apart from the rest. Lewis believed the key was being "merely" Christian and recognizing that we are sinners saved by grace. Screwtape had another idea.

One can list new labels for Christians with a difference prevalent today. You name them—"evangelical," "born-again," "progressive," "liberal," "conservative," and any other political or spiritual label you can imagine.

This is the essence, in my opinion, of Lewis's notion of Christianity. We confuse Christianity with projects, programs, and activities rather than facing the fact that we are sinners due condemnation from a holy and righteous God. Lewis also shows a picture of the church doing exactly the opposite of what it should be doing.

Chapter 26—"Unselfishness vs. Charity"

Screwtape is proud of the work his people have done to substitute the negative word *unselfish* in place of the positive word *charity*. He then goes on to explain how he exploits this idea of unselfishness between the sexes. There follows an amusing example of how people get angry at each other for neither wanting to do what it really wants for fear of being selfish.

Chapter 27—"What Ancient Writers Say"

Screwtape discloses that they have rendered ancient texts—which hold some very important ideas—almost useless because when a "learned man" is asked a question about an old book now, he always refers to the "historical point of view," not whether it is true or false.

Chapter 28—"Wearing Out a Soul"

Screwtape is worried that if the patient is killed tonight, he may lose him to the enemy (God). Screwtape is hoping for a long life because "it is so hard for these creatures to persevere." He is disturbed that the man is being taken out of himself and becoming too dependent on the "enemy." He then describes the list of temptations and disappointments that will wear him down over the years. He wants to wear out a soul by attrition. Even if he is prosperous in his middle years, this is a great opportunity to "knit him to the world."

Chapter 29—"Courage or Cowardice"

In this chapter, Screwtape learns that the Germans will bomb the patient's town. He asks, should they want him to be a coward or courageous with consequent pride or at hatred of the Germans. Screwtape can use any to his father's benefit. Screwtape admits that that his side has not been able to produce any virtue. He laments this fact because to have great wickedness, a man needs some virtue. Attila would have been nothing without his courage.

Chapter 30—"Expectation Equals Entitlement"

The patient's behavior during the air raid has been the worst imaginable from Screwtape's point of view. Screwtape makes a point that is prevalent today—what one comes to expect he soon sees as a right.

Chapter 31—"Death as the Devil Sees It"

The patient "slips through Wormwood's fingers." He is killed in battle, and Screwtape describes the moment of his passing. It is a picture of the devil's greatest fear.

"Screwtape Proposes a Toast"—a prophetic indictment of American education

In 1961, *The Screwtape Letters* was re-released with a new preface and an additional chapter called "Screwtape Proposes a Toast." Lewis's preface to the "Toast" reveals an interesting fact about his motive for writing it. He is pointing out current disturbing trends in education that he saw as most advanced in America. However, the "Toast" was first published in the *Saturday Evening Post*, an American publication; and Lewis thought it neither "good manners nor good tactics" for a foreigner to bring criticism against the American education system. Instead, he has *Screwtape* hold up English education for ridicule.

The predictions of *Screwtape* demonstrated, with uncanny accuracy, the result of these devilish schemes. As we race for equality in all things, we lose something very important—excellence.

The scene is at an annual dinner of the Tempters' Training College. There are complaints about the quality of the souls on which they are "feasting." There are no great sinners present there like a Farinata, a Henry VIII, or a Hitler. The fare was of petty criminals and sinners who were not even sure of their sins. Their quality is inferior, but Screwtape tells the quests to consider the numbers.

Screwtape reveals the key to acquiring this quantity is to misuse the word *democracy*. The trick here is to make the patients move from the idea that democracy means all people should be *treated* equally to the belief that all men *are* equal. Of course, none of us are equal in anything—in size, intellect, talents or kindness.

The idea or feeling is to get the patient to say and think, "I'm as good as you." Lewis contends that this is a lie that is now at the center of a man's being, and it is a great deception because the man himself does not believe it. If he were as good as someone else, he wouldn't have to say it. The "scholar," for instance never says to the "dunce," "I'm as smart as you." Tom Brady would never say to me, "I am as good a quarterback as you are."

Screwtape believes he can get people to do things with pride that under normal or past conditions, they would be ashamed of doing.

All of this leads to a drive for "parity of esteem"—a world where no one can show any excellence or achievement over another, a world where everyone is equal rather than treated equally, a world where no one can be offended, a world of political correctness, a world where what would have been termed sin in the past is not just tolerated but celebrated.

It is Screwtape's goal that "all incentives to learn and all penalties for not learning will disappear." We can see this attitude in places besides education. Incentives for not working, for not following or respecting the law, and for not simply acting civilly are widespread as well.

Lewis summed up the result and danger of an education system built on the "parity of esteem." In an essay, "Democratic Education," when explaining how in this system of education where "no boy, and no boy's parents, need feel inferior," he summed it up well when he wrote that "a nation of dunces can only be safe in a world of dunces."

Screwtape contended that no dictator can stand superiority. Bringing everyone down to the same level is the trick.

As I reread *The Screwtape Letters*, it seemed even more fresh and poignant than the first time I read it thirty years ago. When one considers the cultural, educational, and religious changes that have occurred in that time, some would have seemed impossible then; yet Lewis, through *Screwtape*, predicted it.

"Bodleian Library Oxford"

CHAPTER 5
The Abolition of Man

Lewis said his favorite book but least read was *The Abolition of Man*. I think I know why it was not popular. Although the subject is important—*How Education Develops Man's Sense of Morality*—the method of explanation is exacting and detailed. Lewis gives us his view as to how some of the opinions of theologians, politicians, and educators have evolved due to the removal of absolute truth from education.

The Abolition of Man is the result of three Riddell memorial lectures Lewis gave in February 1943. The three lectures were titled "Men without Chests," "The Way," and "The Abolition of Man"— the names of the three chapters in the book. The complete title is *The Abolition of Man: Reflections on Education with Special Reference to the Teaching of English in the Upper forms of Schools*. The genesis of the lectures and the book was the result of requests to review two English Textbooks. Lewis was asked to review two English books— one written by two Australians, Alex King and Martin Ketley, titled *The Control of Language* (1940); the other by E. G. Biaggini titled *The Reading and Writing of English* (1936). The second book is hardly mentioned in his critique. The first book is criticized in detail, along with its authors.

Lewis had nothing good to say about the Australians' book, but out of courtesy to the authors and the publisher for sending him a complimentary copy, he kept them anonymous. He called the book *The Green Book* (the cover of the book was green), and he named the authors Gaius (*gay-us*) and Titius (*tish-uhs*). He promised it was a real book, and he had it in his library. The book now resides at the

Marion Wade Center at Wheaton College. Lewis called it a little book on English "intended for boys and girls in the upper forms of schools."

Chapter 1—"Men without Chests"

> *The Master said, He who sets forth to work on a different strand destroys the whole fabric.*
> —Confucius, Analects II. 16

With surgical brilliance, Lewis takes one line in *The Green Book* and uses it as the basis for a thorough indictment of the moral relativism (the absence of moral absolutes) that was showing itself in education even in 1943. He went on to explain how this use of moral relativism produces "men without chests."

For centuries, Plato's analogy of the human body was used to explain how morality is formed; he used the head, chest, and stomach of a man as the organs that determine a man's behavior. The head produces reason, and the stomach appetites. The chest controls both by its magnanimity. Lewis contends that the philosophy of *The Green Book* will make "men without chests." Thus, reason and appetites no longer have an organ designed to control them.

As in most all his books, Lewis not only tells you what he believes; he also tells you why he believes it and why the consequences of ignoring the truth, as he sees it, will lead to disaster. This is no more evident than in his book *The Abolition of Man*.

In many of Lewis's works, there is the assumption and the attempt to show the existence of a universal moral law. In *Mere Christianity*, Lewis gives many examples of how different cultures have had moral codes that may have differed, but they were never so different that they amounted to a total difference—a moral code that was almost universally practiced by all cultures at all times. The thesis of this book is that if the "moral law" is removed from education and substituted with a relative moral code, the result will be obvious—the abolition of man, as we know him. This book, in my opinion, is the most prophetic of them all. Simply put, Lewis believed the removal of reason and morality from education would be replaced instead with rule by instinct. Instinct will be unmanageable and consequently fatal. I think this idea is best illustrated by how we phrase the question when soliciting an opinion of someone on a subject. More times than not, we ask, "How do you feel?" about a subject rather than, "What do you think?" about the subject. This may seem like a minor, fine point, but Lewis believes it has major implications.

Lewis calls this moral law or natural law, as he refers to in *The Abolition of Man*, the "Tao." It is the set of moral conduct and obligations that have been written in us as individuals and "forms all moral thought in all its forms, Platonic, Aristotelian, Stoic, Christian, and Oriental alike."

The passage in *The Green Book* from which Lewis launched his attack is a story used by Coleridge of two tourists at a waterfall. One called the waterfall *sublime*, the other *pretty*. Coleridge agreed with the first judgement and rejected the second. Gaius and Titius disagreed with Coleridge and commented as follows:

> When the man said This is sublime, he appeared to be making a remark about the waterfall... Actually ...he was not making a remark about the waterfall, but a remark about his own feelings. What he was saying was really I have feelings associated in my mind with the word "Sublime", or shortly, I have sublime feelings.

Lewis says, setting up his major point, that many deep questions are settled in a quick fashion. Is something really sublime, or is the idea of sublime merely in the mind of the speaker? The authors are not yet finished. They add:

> This confusion is continually present in language as we use it. We appear to be saying something very important about something: and actually we are only saying something about our own feelings.

(Of course, this last statement makes their [Gaius and Titius] statement meaningless because it is, after all, a statement, not about truth but about their own feelings.)

Lewis went on to dismantle the authors' premise. Without all the details recited here, Lewis concluded that the speaker's feelings would not be one of sublimity but rather veneration (great respect). Logically, one would say his feelings are really one of humility. The absurdities of *The Green Book* become evident and comical.

"It would force them to maintain that you are contemptible means I have contemptible feelings…" It does not express the fact that the recipient of the comment is indeed contemptible.

You should read it for yourself. The point, in my opinion, is that *The Green Book* is witness to the natural urge for people to resist truth and to make whatever is happening in the world justified by other factors. It is my emotion or opinion or self-interest that overrides what is right and true. Lewis contends that if we follow *The Green Book*'s logic any statement about morality or value only expresses the emotional state of the speaker and is consequently unimportant.

I don't think it is too far a leap from that logic that helps explain the acceptance of actions which, for centuries, had been regarded as immoral, disrespectful, and laughable. This idea of a relative moral code touches every part of life today—theology, education, politics, art, and sex. Sometimes, these changes are more than tolerated. They are accepted and often celebrated. Morality, like beauty, is now in the eye or the mind of the beholder.

Lewis then tells us how subtly this happens when he critiques the passage further. It is easy to see the importance of what the authors are saying.

> The very power of Gaius and Titius (writers of curricula) depends on the fact that they are dealing with a boy: a boy who thinks he is 'doing' his 'English prep' and has no notion that ethics, theology, and politics are all at stake. It is not a theory they put in his mind but an assumption, which ten years hence, its origin forgotten and

its presence unconscious, will condition him to take one side in a controversy which he has never recognized as a controversy at all. The authors themselves, I suspect, hardly know what they are doing to the boy and he cannot know what is being done to him.

Lewis goes on to point out that there are some immediate practical results. The authors of *The Green Book* use a poorly written advertisement about travel as an example of how advertisers manipulate the reader. Instead of comparing it with well-written passages by great writers, they point out only enough of the work to ridicule the sentiment of patriotism and adventure.

Lewis concludes,

From this passage the schoolboy will learn about literature precisely nothing. What he will learn quickly enough, and perhaps indelibly, is that all emotions aroused by local association are in themselves contrary to reason and contemptible.

At first, Lewis said the authors did not realize what they were doing; but later, he surmised that they may indeed "be intending to make a clean sweep of traditional values and start with a new set."

Lewis proffers the notion that they may have slipped into the idea that of debunking traditional values in order to protect youth from their naive sentiment. But Lewis asserts that

The task of the modern educator is not to cut down jungles but to irrigate deserts. The right defense against false sentiment is to inculcate just sentiments. By starving the sensibility of our pupils we only make them easier prey to the propagandist when he comes. For famished nature will be avenged and a hard heart is no protection against a soft head.

In other words, making someone cynical does not necessarily make one smart.

He went on to say that it was not until recently that "all teachers and even all men believed the universe to be such that certain emotional reactions on our part could be either congruous or incongruous to it." The philosophy of *The Green Book* opens all kinds of possibilities about how we view and value reality. The man who called the cataract (waterfall) sublime was not intending to simply describe his own emotions about it; he was also claiming that the object was one which merited those claims.

This idea also has a devastating effect concerning negative pronouncements. As Lewis pointed out, if I call another contemptible, that means only—if we follow *The Green Book*'s idea—that my feelings are contemptible, not that the person I am addressing is himself contemptable. Any judgement value, whether positive or negative, is meaningless because it is only a reflection of the speaker's feelings.

Not having been in the classroom for decades, I have no way of knowing if this theme has advanced or not. However, judging from some of the outcomes in the arts, law, and religion, it appears we have accepted the philosophy of *The Green Book*, even if by another method or methods.

Chapter 2—"The Way"

> *It is upon the trunk that a gentleman works.*
> *—The Analects of Confucius, 2*

Lewis contended that the practical result of education in the spirit of *The Green Book* is the destruction of the people that accept it. However, Gaius and Titius had a problem. They were skeptical about the Tao and the traditional values, but they were certain about their values. When one says there are no absolute truths or values, they must (it seems odd) accept the statement that there are no absolute truths or values.

Lewis wondered how they would get anyone to follow their values if they were not good values. According to them, the term *good* is only a state of their minds, not an absolute. Consequently, they used terms like *necessary* or *efficient* or *progressive* to get people to accept their assumptions.

There is almost always a cost-benefit analysis used to convince the person the action is "good." One could never make an appeal, for instance, to lay down one's life for his country based on patriotism or honor or valor. After all, these are states of mind, not reality.

In reality, Lewis said, if we cut away the values of the Tao or sentiment or tradition, we are left then with only instinct to guide our actions. But Lewis said quite rightly that when we obey instinct, we are really just obeying people. People say different things. Our instincts are at war. Lewis showed that the authors were "cutting down" old sentiments rather than "irrigating deserts." He called the purveyors of this work on traditional values "an innovator in values." And he said, "It looks, in fact, as if an ethics based on instinct will give the innovator all he wants and nothing that he does not want."

He then noted that without appealing to something higher, we are left with no obvious ways to proceed. Instead, we use words like *basic* or *fundamental* or *primal* or the *deepest instinct*. These words reflect nothing about value but rather intensity.

Lewis then asked the ultimate question. He wondered if there was an instinct that gave us concern for posterity. He admitted it was not found in himself. When we go past the love of a mother to practical planning for the future, we are considering something other than instinct.

Choice and reflection from humans, if their choices are not based in the Tao, can only express what is helpful to those who choose and reflect.

Lewis concluded that without the Tao, there is no morality. However, he realized that the modern mind cannot accept the reality of the Tao and the conclusions he had reached. Lewis speculated the argument against his assertion will be that these absolutes are the result of a "phenomenon" like any other that shall be explained away. Evolutionary ethics is already here.

After he exposed all the arguments, the "innovators" can articulate against his argument for the Tao and against those that "step outside it." He suggested that we can now see what happens to man when we think we have controlled and mastered our environment and are "now master ourselves [who] choose our own destiny."

Chapter 3—"The Abolition of Man"

> *It came burning hot into my mind, whatever he said and however he flattered, when he got me to his house, he would sell me for a slave.*
>
> —Bunyan

If you have read this far in my summary of C. S. Lewis's explanation of the condition of man, I hope you will continue to the end. This chapter, I believe, reveals many things we see happening before our eyes. These things may be a natural progression of human instinct that no one could have changed or perhaps something that could have been avoided if we had merely followed the precepts of the ancient values as reflected in the Tao.

Nevertheless, Lewis's conclusions are shockingly relevant today. First, let us sum up what we have learned so far.

Lewis believed that if the philosophy of *The Green Book* is followed, if we believe there is no real right or wrong or that no objective value has any meaning, we are certain to produce "men without chests"—men and women who are unable to use reason properly or to moderate their appetites. Those who adhere to this logic will then have to devise reasons for people to be motivated to do what is right to manipulate their normal response to any given situation. The 'innovators' will then try to mold man and nature into their own image. In Lewis's view, this work will naturally lead to the abolition of man himself.

Lewis now begins to call the innovators "conditioners." Their goal is to have control over others. Lewis contended that each generation exercises control over the following generations. Just think of the debt our generation is leaving younger generations. Many people, as an example, think man has "licked nature." But in actuality, man's control of nature only means some men's control over other men.

Lewis took the position that every seeming advancement by man which seemingly suggests man's conquest of nature,

...[really] means the rule of a few hundreds of men over billions upon billions of men... Each advance leaves man weaker as well as stronger. In every victory, besides being the general who triumphs, he is also the prisoner who follows the triumphal car.

...The final stage is come when Man by eugenics, by pre-natal conditioning, and by an education and propaganda based on a perfect applied psychology, has obtained full control over himself. Human nature will be the last part of Nature to surrender to man.

Lewis then gave a lengthy list of educationalists who had radical ideas about the raising of children and then gave thanks to the "beneficent obstinacy of real mothers, real nurses, and (above all) real children for preserving the human race in such sanity as it still possesses."

We are then shown the trick of nature. It only appears to be surrendering to our efforts to conquer it.

All Nature's reverses have been but tactical withdrawals. We thought we were beating her back when she was luring us on. What looked to us as hands held up in surrender was really the opening of arms to enfold us forever.

There are critics that will say this line of thought that Lewis expounded is simply an illiterate antiscientific view of the world. However, I believe no one will argue that with each advancement, there almost necessarily comes with it a counter loss. Perhaps, as Lewis ended his book, he was right that he was asking the impossible. But his fear was not so much the advancement of science but the death of reason and morality in the process.

Oxford University Church St Mary the Virgin—Where Lewis
gave his most famous sermon "The Weight of Glory"

CHAPTER 6
The Weight of Glory

During the 1940s, Lewis was in great demand as a speaker. In addition to the broadcast talks that were later made into *Mere Christianity*, he gave talks to the military; he headed up the Socratic Club, a debating society at Oxford; and he preached many sermons. Many agree that his most famous sermon, titled "The Weight of Glory," was given on June 8, 1941 in the Oxford University Church of St. Mary the Virgin. The prose was soaring, the message inspiring, and the ending surprising.

In addition to being published immediately after the sermon was delivered, it was also published in a book by the same name. The book is still in publication. In the book *The Weight of Glory*, there are eight other sermons and essays: "Learning in War-Time," "Why I Am Not a Pacifist," "Transposition," "Is Theology Poetry?," "The Inner Ring," "Membership," "On Forgiveness," and "A Slip Of The Tongue." I am including a short summary of the background and content of the works.

"Learning in War-Time" was preached at the Oxford University Church St. Mary's the Virgin on October 22, 1939. With war just starting between England and Germany, there was obviously much apprehension among the students at Oxford. It was thought that perhaps someone like Lewis, a veteran of World War I and an Oxford Don, could help put the students' position in context and help reassure them that their studies should not be shaken by the imminent threat of serving in the military. He pointed out the obvious, as he always does so well. He claims there are three enemies to learning:

excitement, frustration, and fear. These are not new and are distractions in peacetime as well as war. He cautioned his listeners not to let their situation seem more abnormal than it really was. All these enemies of learning were always there; it is just that war made them acute. War makes these things real to us.

"Why I Am Not a Pacifist" was given as a talk to a pacifist society at Oxford sometime in 1940. This is more evidence that Lewis did not fear to express views that were unpopular to his audience. His appeal in this address was to logic and began by defining the terms discussed very specifically. He took the argument to its logical conclusion. Those countries that allowed pacifists in large enough numbers would soon be controlled by countries who did not allow pacifists, and that would quickly mean a world with no pacifists at all. Lewis's brilliance is always underpinned by uncommon common sense.

"Transposition" was preached at Mansfield College, Oxford. It was given on May 28, 1944. It was reported that Lewis became emotional during the sermon and had to remove himself from the pulpit. He came back later after a hymn was sung and finished the sermon. Lewis contends in the sermon that the spiritual is greater than the material existence we observe.

"Is Theology Poetry?" was read to the Oxford University Socratic Club on November 6, 1944. The question Lewis was asked to debate as he restated it was this: Does Christian theology owe its attraction to its power of arousing and satisfying our imagination? Lewis contended that as poetry, the doctrine of the Trinity was nowhere near his idea of effective poetry. Lewis said in the paper that he liked Greek mythology much better and Irish and Norse best of all. One of Lewis's most-often quoted lines is in this paper. It is the last sentence. He likened Christianity to the sun when it rises. He knew it was there not because he could see it but because with its light, he could see everything else. His reason for the statement was simple and radical: Christian theology, he said, fits into every other discipline—science, art, morality, and the sub-Christian religions—whereas the scientific point of view cannot fit into any of these studies, not even science itself.

Lewis then gives a fascinating view of the scientific explanation for life. It is far more appealing from a poetic standpoint than the Christian view of life. Lewis contends that the mystery of that view of life appeals more to the imagination than the Christian view. It is also worth reading.

"The Inner Ring" was given as a speech at Kings College, University of London on December 14, 1944. It was for the school's Commemoration Oration. Lewis opens the speech by quoting Tolstoy's *War and Peace*. It shows the realization of one of the characters in the novel that there existed different kinds of relationships. The character wanted to be in the "inner circle," which was not the part of the normal line of authority. It is a natural urge that can be dangerous—to be part of a group for any purpose. The important thing is friendship for the right reasons, not for what will help you. Lewis was, in many professional circles, excluded because of his Christian beliefs but more importantly his Christian writings and proclamations.

"Membership" is a paper that proclaims the need for believers to gather in corporate worship. It was read to the Society of St. Alban and St. Sergius, Oxford on February 10, 1945.

"On Forgiveness" was published after Lewis's death. It was to appear in a publication in 1947 in a church publication. That did not happen and was later discovered by Mr. Walter Hooper in 1975 at the Bodleian Library in Oxford.

"A Slip of the Tongue" was the last sermon preached by Lewis. It was delivered at the chapel at Magdalene College, Cambridge.

The following is the sermon "The Weight of Glory" and the major points it expresses. Many regard it as Lewis's greatest prose.

"The Weight of Glory"

The circumstances of the sermon "The Weight of Glory," just as those of the broadcast talks, were very similar. Lewis was explaining and defending the Gospel of Christ in the most unlikely of times with the most unlikely of messages. In 1941, England was facing the worst of the German assault against England. Thousands in London and the rest of England had been killed by indiscriminate bombing. While Hitler was having his way, Lewis was talking about heaven and *our* responsibilities for other's *glory*. It is worth noting that the best of Lewis's apologetic works were done during the darkest times of British history.

Lewis does three very important things in this sermon. First, he dispels the idea that it is somehow mercenary or selfish to desire heaven; instead, Lewis insists it is the proper reward and natural consummation of our activity as Christians. Second, through some of his most eloquent prose, he describes the longing we all feel and desire but that which we can never quite obtain. He also paints a glorious picture of what heaven may be like. Third, as any good writer, he turns the tables on the reader and makes sure we are not too concerned with our own glory.

Lewis sets the stage by asking the following question about how we view love and unselfishness. He suggests that a positive term (love) is replaced by a negative one (unselfishness). (Unselfishness suggests going without; love suggests giving.) Lewis notes that we are indeed asked to bear our cross and follow him. However, everything that results from the following of *our Captain* meets all our desires. Lewis says that those who worry about us wanting too much are completely misguided. As you will see, Lewis maintains the exact opposite is true.

God, says Lewis, sees our desires as too weak and not too strong. We are always being tripped up by things like drinks, sex, and ambition when perfect joy is offered to us.

The greatest things we experience here on earth still, in the final analysis, do not satisfy. As St. Augustine put it, "Our heart is restless until it rests in thee." Lewis admitted in this sermon that he was trying to weave a spell, but he said that it is true that spells are used for breaking enchantments as well as casting them.

The way he describes our longing for heaven is worth the read. We have a desire in us for something we cannot quite name, and we have nothing in our current experience to attach that desire to.

Lewis also acknowledges that the realization of the desire for heaven and appreciation of the Gospel over the Law is a slow process. The realization is almost unnoticeable just as a tide lifts boats.

In his opinion, the education system is constantly trying to weave a spell of worldliness on its pupils. It is trying to still that small, quiet voice.

In the first portion of the sermon, Lewis compared the lack of desire for heaven in us like the schoolboy who is first learning his Greek, not realizing how wonderful it will be to read Greek poetry one day in Greek or his adult enjoyment of reading Sophocles. He cannot look at those things (Greek literature) as a lover looks toward marriage and a general toward victory as the proper reward for the activity. Likewise, we do not see the immediate reward of heaven.

Lewis makes the distinction between proper rewards and improper ones. A man marrying for money does not have the proper reward of marriage. A general who is paid for his victory is a mercenary and does not have the proper reward for his victory.

Love for the man who marries and victory for the general who wins are the proper rewards and are a natural ending to a proper effort.

Lewis describes the schoolboy as working for good marks or avoiding punishment when he begins his Greek. The benefit of the Greek lessons dawn on him slowly. It is the same with our recognition of heaven.

Lewis here alludes to his first reluctance to accept and repulsion at the Christian promise of "glory" hereafter. He also tells us that this process of the realization of our true destination is a slow one. It is not surprising then that since we are made for heaven, the desire for our proper place had nothing to attach itself to at first; and anything around us that we try to attach to this longing can only be symbolic and is consequently not the thing itself.

Lewis also said it is almost impossible for us to express our longing because we have not yet experienced it, nor can we hide it because we want it so much. He also pointed out that there is nothing in our experience that can satisfy the joy and longing we desire; the things we thought gave them only came through them.

Perhaps, at best, is a reflection of the source of joy. Longing came through them. The longing that the things themselves cannot satisfy demonstrates Lewis's eloquence and at the same time his ability to make a hard subject easier to understand. In the words prior to this part of "The Weight of Glory," after the most beautiful of his prose, he acknowledged his goal. Lewis asked the readers if they thought he was trying to weave a spell. He believed the education system has cast the worst spell of all, trying to still that "small, quiet voice" that, in Lewis's opinion, tells us this is not our home. But he said spells are used to induce enchantments as well as dispel them.

Lewis maintained that our whole system of education has been used to argue that all the good man can achieve is on this earth. Even though we accomplish all we want here on earth, what we have will be eventually lost. We will lose it for no other reason than the sun will burn out and the entire universe will wind down. In any event, life as we know it will cease to exist; history will end.

When Lewis first became a Christian, he was dismissive of and uninterested in the promise of glory and heaven. He thought of it as either fame or luminosity—the first being evil and the second ridiculous. Glory, in our human experience, is a competitive idea. Luminosity was a comical idea to him. He compared it to being kind of a living electric light bulb. However, after looking closer at the idea of glory, he found a different meaning.

When he began to study the idea of glory, he was amazed how many Christians of old agreed that this glory was more in the meaning of good report or approval—approval by God, not approval or fame given to us by others. Lewis compared it to the approval of a superior to an inferior, a master to a servant, a teacher to a student, and a parent to a child.

Lewis said he had missed the point due to his pride. He finally saw that this type of approval was the most basic of all emotions.

And then Lewis said he realized that what he thought he wanted was keeping him from seeing what God had planned.

This idea of Lewis echoes the sentiment Lewis expressed at his conversion to theism. The things that God "compels" us to do are the things that "liberate" us.

Lewis pointed out that being accepted by God is part of the "inconsolable secret" that has been haunting us. After explanations of us passing through nature to the reality behind nature, we will see God because even nature is mortal. We finally see what is behind everything we have experienced in this life. We are finally face-to-face with him and consequently filled with pure and perfect joy.

Then, as all good writers do, he turns the table on the reader. Lewis, in my opinion, in the closing of "The Weight of Glory," expressed in some of his greatest prose what the consequences of Christian belief are. They are far more than the words we recite almost mindlessly each Sunday. They are more than even our service and talents. The great lesson we learn from Lewis about our faith is that we express grand ideas that we say we believe. But how do we live them out? As always, Lewis took these beliefs to their logical conclusion when it comes to heaven as well. See what you think "The Weight of Glory" really means.

Lewis asks us to think not about our glory but rather our neighbor's. It is their potential glory that is the burden we should carry. Every person we meet is not ordinary but a soul that will live forever. With everyone we meet, we are helping that person to either heaven (*glory*) or separation from God (*hell*).

Although I miss the mark much more often than not, Lewis's idea that we are dealing with immortals every day has changed my view of the people I meet and hopefully my conduct and attitude toward them. There is also an unpleasant side in realizing the consequences of our belief. Our charity (love) must be real and cost us something, not a parity of love. It must be more than tolerance. It is hard, almost impossible, to be honest with a neighbor and a close friend or family member; yet if we see them as immortal, we can do no less. If they are immortal, we are helping them to one place or the other each day.

The Eagle and Child aka "The Bird and Baby"—
where the Inklings met for lunch on Tuesdays

CHAPTER 7

Postscript and Other Works

In 1955, Lewis accepted an academic chair created for him at the Magdalene College, Cambridge. It was the position of professor of Medieval and Renaissance literature. Despite his fame and acknowledged accomplishments or perhaps because of them, Lewis had not been given an academic chair after twenty-five years at Oxford. An Oxford or Cambridge chair would mean no more individual tutorials. The tutorials were very time-consuming. It is astounding that he kept up his tutorial obligations and at the same time was able to produce such a prolific amount of literary works.

In his inaugural address at Cambridge, he admitted that he was a dying breed of males. He called them and himself the "Old-Western men." As I conclude this book on Lewis, I am sure many of the ideas, beliefs, and morals that he expressed and I have made known make us both look like the dinosaur Lewis described in his Cambridge address. He felt like a dinosaur mainly due to the changes he was seeing in education. I suspect he would be astounded at the changes inside and outside of education in the last sixty-plus years since that address. But Lewis said we (us dinosaurs) are worth examination.

In his talk, Lewis used the picture of a live dinosaur dragging itself through a classroom. He talked about looking back as he fled just to see what it really looked like. And he would give anything to talk to an ancient Athenian, no matter how ignorant he may be. Lewis acknowledged he was like the Athenian. He may not be useful as a critic but he may be useful as a specimen. He acknowledged you will not see any more like him (Lewis).

For certain, we will not see the likes of him again. In fact, it is almost impossible for the current education and political environment to produce such a scholar and writer. Fortunately, we have his remains, in the form of his books, to study and enjoy.

The works of C. S. Lewis are so expansive that it is hard to focus on just a few of his books without missing the overall body of his work. His work is so diverse that sometimes it is hard to see the connection in all his efforts. There is a common message in his work, though. There is a God who is working for his purpose and his glory, no matter how strange it may appear to us.

I have learned that many like me treasure his apologetics, the logical defense, and the explanation of traditional Christian belief. Others like his science fiction. Many more enjoy the children's stories. His scholarly works are less-read but just as important.

Whatever you enjoy, you will find the same theme—sometimes obvious, sometimes "smuggled" in his work.

I am finishing this book by giving a summary of the books and essays that helped me the most. One thing is certain. In all his works the same themes recur in each book or essay—homage to an all-powerful, all-knowing, merciful Creator.

The Problem of Pain. Published in 1940, it is the first "straight" work of Christian defense he ever wrote. If you read nothing else, the preface and introduction are worth the price of the book.

God in the Dock: Essays on Theology and Ethics. First published in 1970, there are forty-eight essays in this book. Here are a few I particularly liked:

- "Answers to Questions on Christianity"
- "Myth Became Fact"
- "Man or Rabbit"
- "What Are We to Make of Jesus Christ?"
- "God in the Dock"
- "The Humanitarian Theory of Punishment"

The Chronicles of Narnia. There are seven books in this series. The most famous is *The Lion, the Witch, and the Wardrobe.* Many of Lewis's apologetic views are reinforced and "smuggled in" (as Lewis put it) in these books. The books were published between 1950 and 1956. All are still in print.

The Weight of Glory and Other Addresses. Not to be confused with the sermon of the same title, although it does include the sermon. It is a book with a collection of sermons. Some of my favorites are the following:

- "The Weight of Glory"
- "Learning in War-Time"
- "Why I am Not a Pacifist"
- "Is Theology Poetry"
- "On Forgiveness"

Miracles. This book was first published in 1947. It is an explanation of how God intervenes in nature and human affairs.

Reflection on the Psalms. The introduction in the book is worth the cost. The introduction should be mandatory for the clergy. It was first published in 1958.

The Space Trilogy. *Out of the Silent Planet, Prelandra,* and *That Hideous Strength* were published in this order, beginning in 1938 and the last publication in 1945.

A Grief Observed. Published in 1960, Lewis first published it under another name. It is the description of his grief following his wife's death.

Important Dates in the Life of C. S. Lewis

- 1898—Born in Belfast, Ireland on November 29
- 1908—Lewis's mother, Florence, dies of cancer on August 23
- 1908—Sent to boarding school at Wynyard in England in 1910, attends Campbell College in Ireland
- 1911—Enters Malvern College

- 1914—Goes to Surrey England and is tutored by W. T. Kirkpatrick
- 1917—Begins study at University College, Oxford
- 1918—Wounded in action in World War I
- 1922—Graduates from Oxford
- 1925—Elected Fellow English Literature at Magdalen College, Oxford.
- 1929—Father Albert J. Lewis dies. Lewis accepts the existence of God
- 1931—Professes belief in Jesus Christ
- 1941—Begins series of talks on the BBC
- 1942—Publishes *The Screwtape Letters*
- 1950—Publishes *The Lion, the Witch, and the Wardrobe*
- 1955—Becomes Professor at Magdalene College Cambridge
- 1956—Marries Joy Gresham in a civil ceremony
- 1957—Marries Gresham in an Anglican ceremony
- 1963—Dies on November 22, along with Aldous Huxley and John F. Kennedy

About the Author

Bob Hereford is a native of Waycross, Georgia where he stills resides. He and his wife Patricia have two sons and seven grandchildren.

In 1988, while on vacation in Fernandina Beach, Florida, he bought the only religious book available in a local bookstore. That week, he read *Mere Christianity* by C. S. Lewis and thus began a thirty-one-year journey into the study of one of the twentieth-century's greatest Christian apologists. As a result, he has spoken in churches for more than twenty-five years about the life and works of Lewis. Included in his presentation is a characterization of Lewis from *Mere Christianity*, complete with a British accent.

He is an active member of the Trinity United Methodist Church in Waycross.

Bob has worked in the insurance industry as an agent and consultant for nearly fifty years and attended the University of Georgia and the Valdosta State University.